T0375742

Ladybird Readers

What Is This Shape?

To access the audio and digital versions
of this book:

1 Go to **www.ladybirdeducation.co.uk**
2 Click "Unlock book"
3 Enter the code below

VeJvuqh76U

Notes to teachers, parents, and carers

The **Ladybird Readers** Beginner level helps young language learners to become familiar with key conversational phrases in English. The language introduced has clear real-life applications, giving children the tools to hold their first conversations in English.

This book focuses on introducing basic shapes in English, and provides practice of asking and answering a question beginning with "What is..."

There are some activities to do in this book. They will help children practice these skills:

 Speaking   Listening*   Reading

*To complete these activities, listen to the audio downloads available at **www.ladybirdeducation.co.uk**

Series Editor: Sorrel Pitts
Chants by Sorrel Pitts

LADYBIRD BOOKS

UK | USA | Canada | Ireland | Australia
India | New Zealand | South Africa

Ladybird Books is part of the Penguin Random House group of companies
whose addresses can be found at global.penguinrandomhouse.com.
www.penguin.co.uk   www.puffin.co.uk   www.ladybird.co.uk

Penguin
Random House
UK

Text inspired by *Little Cloud* by Eric Carle, first published in Great Britain by Hamish Hamilton, 1997
This version first published by Ladybird Books 2024
001

Text and illustrations copyright © Penguin Random House LLC, 1996
Adapted text and artwork copyright © 2024 by Penguin Random House LLC
The moral right of the original author/illustrator has been asserted

ERIC CARLE'S name and signature logotype and the World of Eric Carle logo are trademarks of Penguin Random House LLC.
This edition published by arrangement with World of Eric Carle, an imprint of Penguin Young Readers Group, a division of Penguin Random House LLC.
All rights reserved including the right of reproduction in whole or in part in any form.
To find out more about Eric Carle and his books, please visit eric-carle.com. To learn about The Eric Carle Museum of Picture Book Art, please visit carlemuseum.org.

Printed in China

The authorized representative in the EEA is Penguin Random House Ireland, Morrison Chambers, 32 Nassau Street, Dublin D02 YH68

A CIP catalogue record for this book is available from the British Library

ISBN: 978–0–241–58772–0

All correspondence to:
Ladybird Books
Penguin Random House Children's
One Embassy Gardens, 8 Viaduct Gardens, London SW11 7BW

MIX
Paper | Supporting
responsible forestry
FSC® C018179

What Is This Shape?

Inspired by
Little Cloud
by Eric Carle

What is this shape?

It is a square.

What is this shape?

It is a circle.

What is this shape?

It is a triangle.

What is this shape?

It is a rectangle.

What is this shape?

It is an oval.

Your turn!

1 Listen. Circle the words.

1   oval   (triangle)

2   square   circle

3   rectangle   triangle

4   square   circle

2 **Read the sentences. Match.**

1 It is a rectangle.

2 It is a circle.

3 It is an oval.

4 It is a triangle.

3 Read and clap!

What is this shape?
It is a square! It is a square!

What is this shape?
It is a circle! It is a circle!

What is this shape?
It is a triangle! It is a triangle!

What is this shape?
It is a rectangle! It is a rectangle!

What is this shape?
It is an oval! It is an oval!

I love shapes. I love shapes!